IF GOD IS GOOD...?

Tragedy, God's Sovereignty, and the Solution to the Problem of Evil

DAVID A. HOLLAND

"If God is Good … ?"
Tragedy, God's Sovereignty, and the Solution to the Problem of Evil

Copyright © 2023 David A. Holland

Book design by LynnCreative

ISBN 979-8-9885500-3-7 (PDF/print)
ISBN 979-8-9885500-1-3 (digital/eBook)

DavidAHolland.com

CONTENTS

INTRODUCTION

On March 11, 2011, at 2:46 in the afternoon in Japan, earthquake sensors all over the planet started going bonkers. Seconds earlier, an event seismologists call a *megathrust earthquake* measuring 9.1 on the Richter Scale occurred roughly 45 miles east of the Oshika Peninsula. You don't have to be a seismologist to deduce that any flavor of earthquake with "megathrust" in its name is not a good thing.

It wasn't. In fact, it was the most powerful earthquake ever recorded in Japan, and that's saying something. The force of the tectonic plate shift on the ocean floor yanked the entire main island of Japan, Honshu, roughly eight feet eastward in just a couple of minutes. It shifted the Earth on its axis by estimates of between four and ten inches.

Oh, and as you may recall, it unleashed hell in the form of a tsunami—a wall of water traveling toward the east coast of northern Japan at around 435 miles per hour and, in places, reaching an estimated height of 130 feet. Residents of the Sendai region of Japan got roughly an eight-minute warning to find higher ground. But for many, "higher" wasn't high enough. Countless people managed to reach one of the many tsunami evacuation centers scattered throughout the region but died anyway when more than 100 of these centers were scraped away by a wall of seawater, cars, and shattered buildings.

Over the next few days, a horrified world watched as hundreds of mobile phone videos of the tsunami and its aftermath appeared online and in newscasts. The horror was justified. One study put the death toll at nearly 20,000 with more than 6,000 injured. Four years after the event more than a quarter of a million people still hadn't returned to their homes. Many never will.

This high-profile catastrophe did the two things all high-profile catastrophes do. First, it prompted an immediate outpouring of sympathy and efforts to deliver aid and relief. Then it prompted a "tsunami" of armchair philosophers and online theologians opining, attacking, defending, and explaining where God was or wasn't while all this misery was being unleashed.

There is nothing new about this (with the exception of the online part.) As long as bad things have been happening, there have been people trying to explain why. Especially when those bad things happen to good people.

We're about to tackle one of the most difficult but important subjects on the planet. One that has been sorely vexing philosophers, theologians, and other large-brained humans for thousands of years.

Philosophers call it "the problem of evil." Theologians call their explanations *theodicy*. Us regular people just call it something like: "If God is good and loves people, why are tragedy, misery, and heartache constantly raining down on them in the world?" Getting to a satisfying answer to that question will require waltzing into a theological minefield. Namely, the issue of God's "sovereignty." But hang in here with me and I think you'll come away with an understanding that is not only comforting and life-giving, but it will also move you closer to God.

1

JOB'S KNOW-IT-ALL FRIENDS

The oldest book in the Bible to wrestle with the question of *Why do bad things happen to good people?* is the book of Job. I said the oldest, not the first. The books of the Bible aren't chronological, so Job sits right in the middle.

Each of Job's three friends had an elaborately constructed theological explanation for the epic crap storm they were watching their friend go through. They argued their hypotheses eloquently. They presented them forcefully. But at the end of the book, we find God Almighty lining them up, verbally pulling their pants down, and drawing the word "LOSER" on their foreheads with a Sharpie. (See: Job 42:7–9)

It appears God was insufficiently impressed with their theological arguments. Even so, from then until now, religious folks have been irresistibly drawn to making sense of tragedy. (Dr. Moth, meet Flame. Flame . . . this is Dr. Moth. You two should get together.)

> As the poet Alexander Pope observed several hundred years ago, "Fools rush in where angels fear to tread."

Nevertheless, a cluster of personal events around the same time as the Japanese tsunami got me thinking and reading and praying deeply about this question. For one thing, the long-time administrative assistant for the Senior Pastor of the church I was attending back then died quite suddenly. We'd known Judy for pretty much all of her tenure as the administrative hub of one of the fastest growing churches in America. In excellent health, she picked up a nasty strain of E. coli in something she ate. This led to a cascade of catastrophic health events that ended in her passing away less than a week after falling ill.

At pretty much the same time, a young man at my daughters' high school, a senior, active in his church and a worship leader in his youth group, died after having spent a couple of months in a deep coma resulting from some sort of previously undiagnosed aneurysm.

Luke, like Judy, was a good person. Bad stuff happened to them. And everyone who knew and loved them had … questions.

2

DEFENDING A GOD WHO DOESN'T NEED TO BE DEFENDED

As I said, tragedy tends to bring out the armchair theologian in many. And I understand why. For one thing, that's when we're most likely to hear people impugning God's character. We hear questions uttered like, "If there is, as you Christians claim, a benevolent God in charge of the universe, how is it that He allows things like this to happen?"

Or we hear others using the opportunity to reject the faith altogether. Back in 2011, my daughter told me several of her fellow students at her Christian school had announced that they no longer believed in God because of what happened to their classmate.

Now, we Christians really like God. So much so we have chosen to align our whole lives with His cause. He's the head of our "tribe." We want others to join the tribe as well. So when people start talking trash about Him, or simply walking away from Him, we understandably tend to rush to His defense.

On top of this, we're moved by another very human tendency. One rooted in our insecurities.

We often feel personally offended when someone rejects the thing upon which we've built our entire lives. So when people start saying ugly things about God, we tend to charge in and passionately defend Him. (But what we're really defending is *our* choice.) We can't resist the urge to become God's PR agent—explaining Him and improving His public image.

Of course, this requires addressing thorny theological issues like The Fall, the nature and scope of God's sovereignty, and how to reconcile that sovereignty with Man's free will, (if free will is even a thing!) I say that last part because there are a good number of theologians, philosophers, and theoretical physicists who don't think it is. There are those in all three disciplines who view free will as an illusion.

These are questions with which Christendom's best minds have been grappling since the first century. Yet faced with a doubter or a skeptic pointing to tragedy, few believers can resist rushing in to explain it all in two minutes or less. *Clarissa Explains it All* was the title of a popular show on Nickelodeon back in the nineties. I think of that show every time someone posts something angry about a tragedy on social media and hundreds of "Clarissas" feel compelled to "help" by making sense of it for them.

Here's the problem with all of that. First of all, God is not insecure. His self-esteem is not fragile. And He's been handling rejection with grace and patience for quite a long time now. Sometimes when the doubters and fist shakers get really fierce and feisty, God even finds it amusing:

> *Why do the nations rage and the peoples plot in vain? The kings of the earth set themselves, and the rulers take counsel together, against the Lord and against his Anointed ... He who sits in the heavens laughs ...* (PSALM 2:1-2, 4, ESV)

Furthermore, doubters and pointy-headed skeptics are rarely won over by intellectual arguments (although Paul attempted this at Mars Hill with mixed success.) The Bible makes it pretty clear that our primary weapons of persuasion are these:

Love. And *Power.*

Our trouble is that the brand of Christianity most of the American church displays right now is somewhat deficient in one or both of these commodities.

Finally, I think most Christians have a deeply flawed, overly simplistic view of God's sovereignty. When they go to explain tragedy to doubters and cranks, they simply don't know what they're talking about.

I believe this pervasive and flawed view of God's sovereignty keeps most Christians from praying as often and as effectively as God intended. And I suspect it is turning a whole generation of postmodern young people away from God.

"So, Dave," you're probably saying, "enlighten us. Where has most of the Church gone wrong?" I'll give it my best shot!

3

THE BASHIR-BELL PARADOX

On March 15, 2011, just four days after the Japanese tsunami, pastor-author Rob Bell appeared on MSNBC to be interviewed by Martin Bashir about his new, controversial book, *Love Wins: A Book About Heaven, Hell, and the Fate of Every Person Who Ever Lived*. A segment of that interview instantly went viral.

I don't intend to address the central controversy surrounding Bell's book here. (And trust me, there was controversy.) It's off topic. I mention it only because the opening question Bashir asked Bell strikes at the heart of what I *do* want to tackle. Right out of the gate, Bashir—a crafty interviewer who had previously interviewed Michael Jackson, Princess Diana, and many other notable names—framed a question that encapsulated that age-old "If God is good ..." problem of evil thing.

Here's Bashir's question to Bell:

"Before we talk about the book, just help us with this tragedy in Japan. Which of these is true? God is all-powerful but doesn't care about the people of Japan, and therefore they're suffering.

Or ... He **does** care about the people of Japan but is not all-powerful.

Which one is it?"[1]

Here Bashir does a pretty clever job of concisely summarizing the logical conundrum that has plagued thinkers for centuries and, in recent years, caused hundreds of thousands of young people raised in Christian homes to abandon the faith of their parents.

As a parent of three grown millennials, I've heard my girls talk about numerous friends at their Christian high schools and Christian colleges who were questioning everything about their faith as a direct result of grappling with this "if God is sovereign" … "problem of evil" thing.

For decades, media mogul Ted Turner pointed to the slow, painful death of his sister when he was a boy as the justification for his agnosticism and hostility toward Christianity. (In fairness, Turner softened his rhetoric and apologized in his final years of life.)

4

IF THERE IS A LOVING GOD...?

Several generations of postmodern individuals are traveling Bashir's road of logic. They say, in essence:

> "You Christians tell me that God exists
> and that He loves all mankind. Have you
> looked around? How can you reconcile
> mass starvation, human trafficking,
> state-sponsored torture, war, and
> tsunamis with your concept of God?"

As with Bashir's question posed to Rob Bell, there is a certain logical tidiness to the question. The problem is that all logical constructs stand upon some presuppositions (i.e., assumptions, premises, or "givens").

A logical argument can actually be airtight, but if only one of the assumptions underlying it is false, *sound* logic leads you to a *false* conclusion. For example:

If one presupposes that the earth is flat, it is quite logical to be nervous about sailing too far in one direction, lest one falls off the edge. That's sound logic built upon a flawed assumption. The insidious thing about presuppositions is that they tend to remain buried in our worldview—unexamined and unquestioned. The fact is, the very reason that we have

Liberals and Conservatives;
Republicans and Democrats;
AOC and MTG;
Alec Baldwin and Adam Baldwin

. . . is not because half the population is irrational or crazy. In the vast majority of cases, two people who disagree are both reaching logical and reasonable positions built upon differing and largely unexamined presuppositions they hold to be true.

Everything I've said up to this point has been preparation. Now it's time to solve this puzzle.

5

THE "BRUCE ALMIGHTY" MODEL

Underlying the doubts of most of today's skeptics is a key assumption about God:

> God gets *exactly* what He wants in every
> spot on earth in every second of every day.

This is what Bashir meant when he used the term "all-powerful." The vast majority of Americans—Christian and otherwise—assume the answer is "Yes." This is basically the American, pop culture, Hollywood sitcom concept of God—pulling all the strings, hands on all the levers, including the levers of human action and choice.

In the movie *Bruce Almighty*, Jim Carrey's title character gets to become "God" for a couple of weeks. As a result, he finds himself with the power to make anything he desires happen, including the power to take control of a rival's body and force him to make a fool of himself on camera.

This Hollywood view of God as having unlimited freedom of action on the earth—the belief that everything is playing out just as He has ordained right down to the granular level of the child molestations that are almost certainly happening in various places around the planet as you read these words—is shared by most American Christians who simply haven't thought too deeply about these questions.

We're taught that God is "sovereign." And, as the Bible makes clear, He is. But most of us go on to define that sovereignty in the cartoonish Hollywood terms described above.

This view fails to properly build upon three fundamental, true presuppositions. Remember, assumptions must actually be true if your logic is going to build to a valid conclusion. Those three assumptions are:

1. The Fall
2. Free Will
3. God's Self-Limiting Integrity

In my humble view, neo-Calvinists have a good handle on point one, and their Arminian brethren across the aisle have an important grasp on point two. But there is no major tribe out there championing point three.

To hear many Christians talk about God's sovereignty, you get the impression that Romans 8:28 contains a period after the word *things*, i.e., "And we know that God causes all things."

Of course, there is no period there. The verse says, *"And we know that God causes all things to work together for good to those who love God, to those who are called according to His purpose."* (NASB) That's something *very* different.

One of the unique characteristics of us humans is our capacity for cognitive dissonance—that is, the ability to hold two completely incompatible and conflicting beliefs simultaneously. Thus, it shouldn't surprise us to observe that most evangelical Christians will answer a robust "Yes" to *both* of the following questions:

1. Does God give humans free will ... the ability to choose or reject God's expressed will?
2. Does God's "sovereignty" mean that "everything happens for a reason" and that God either causes or permits every event at every moment in every place on earth as part of His plan?

A little bit of logical pondering will reveal that both propositions cannot possibly be true.

I'm convinced a flawed, simplistic view of God's sovereignty is robbing believers of much of the motivation to pray and the ability to pray effectively. Even worse, it's needlessly causing entire generations of people to dismiss Christianity's message of a loving God who sent His Son to die for a sinful world. (See: Martin Bashir's question to Rob Bell.)

I was a debater back in my college days and therefore know how to argue two different sides of a proposition. If pressed, I could easily cite scripture to support either one of the above questions.

On one hand, there are dozens of Bible verses and stories that make explicit Man's freedom to reject God's will and go his own way. "*Choose* this day who you will

serve ..." Joshua challenged the Israelites. (Joshua 24:15)
Jesus Himself said:

> *"Jerusalem, Jerusalem, who kills the*
> *prophets and stones those who are sent to*
> *her! How often I wanted to gather your*
> *children together, the way a hen gathers*
> *her chicks under her wings, **and you were***
> ***unwilling.*** (MATTHEW 23:37, NASB, EMPHASIS MINE)

Well, looky there! The word "will" is camped right there in the middle of the last word in Jesus' sentence!

On the other hand, many scriptures speak of God's infinite power to produce His desired outcomes. He "declares the end before the beginning." (Isaiah 46:10) Indeed, Paul devotes the entire ninth chapter of Romans—in the course of trying to help the church at Rome (and us) understand how to think about the Jewish people in the wake of the cross—to declaring that God gets the outcomes He wants.

So, which is it? Free will? Or God gets what He wants?

The answer is: Yes.

I'm satisfied that a proper, biblical understanding of how things currently work in the universe can reconcile this "seemingly" irreconcilable dilemma. (And do so without requiring either cognitive dissonance or just throwing one's hands up in the air and saying, "It's a paradox!") To be frank, many Calvinist efforts to deal with "the problem of evil"—the theological term is *theodicy*—end up essentially saying, "Your brain is too little to understand it, so stop trying."

As I mentioned previously, making sense of all this requires an understanding of three things:

1. The Fall (of both Man and Creation)
2. Free Will (and God's corresponding delegation of dominion authority over Creation to Man)
3. God's Self-Limiting Integrity (or Righteousness)

It would take a much longer book to completely unpack these three elements (and I may just write that book someday) but, in short, the Genesis account shows us God legally (covenantally) delegating authority, rights, and responsibilities to Man over the earth:

God blessed them; and God said to them,
"Be fruitful and multiply, and fill the
*earth, and subdue it; **and rule** over the*
fish of the sea and over the birds of the sky
and over every living thing that moves on
the earth." (GENESIS 1:28, NASB, EMPHASIS MINE)

This is a delegation of stewardship authority accompanied by a dominion mandate and takes us to the second reality in our three-part list—The Fall—which subjected both Mankind and all of Nature to some pretty ugly effects.

Since that day, lots of bad things have been happening on this planet. Many of those bad things are the product of evil choices made by fallen people. Other bad things are the result of a curse-wracked creation groaning for a form of redemption and restoration itself.

So WHY, after things got so horribly fouled up ... God being God and all ... did He not immediately jump in and hit the "Undo" button? Or the "Fix It" button? Or simply blow the whole thing up and start again?

The answer lies in the third item on this list: God's Self-Limiting Integrity.

God is holy, righteous, and, above all, good. Given His character, He could not possibly create a universe built upon righteous law and covenantal principle and then toss all that aside when those laws and covenants got inconvenient. That's something *I'd* do.

Instead, God initiated a multi-thousand-year plan to bring about the restoration and renewal of both Man and Nature (chronicled as the Bible's "scarlet thread of redemption".)

. . . a plan that scrupulously followed the rules and laws established before the very beginning. It was a brilliant plan that didn't violate God's legal delegation of authority and dominion to Man.

There's an old freshman theology brain teaser that asks, "Can God make a rock so big He can't move it?"

The truth is, nothing can limit God *except* His own character. God is *self-limited* by His goodness and justness. That is why there is no period after the word "things" in Romans 8:28. God does not "cause all things." But He is so smart, so powerful, and so unimaginably creative, that despite all the bad things put in motion by our choices, an outlaw enemy, and a fallen creation, God still brilliantly, joyfully "causes all things to work together" for our good. **He's *that* smart.**

> In fact, God is smart enough and knows us well enough to know how each of us would choose, of our own free will, in any and every possible set of circumstances.

> Understanding how every person would choose in advance of the actual choice being made gives Him perfect "foreknowledge."

Did you know there's actually an example of this in the Bible? In 1 Samuel chapter twenty-three, David is holed up in the walled Philistine city of Keilah while King Saul has people all over the country searching for him in order to kill him. While there, David gets word that Saul has discovered his hiding spot. So David borrows the "ephod" from the priest Abiathar and starts "inquiring of the Lord" about his sticky situation. First, he asks how

Saul will choose. "Is he really going to choose to come after me here?" David asks. "Yes, he will," God answers.

Based on that answer, David's follow up is: "IF I remain here, will the people of this town betray me to Saul when he comes?" Again, God's answer is "Yes." Armed with that information, David and his men slip out of town before Saul and his forces arrive.

Here's what I want you to see about this incident. In answering David's second question, God obviously wasn't revealing the future. That betrayal by the people of Keilah never happened. At the moment of David's inquiry, there were two *possible* future timelines based on an A/B *choice* that was in David's "free will" hands.

In timeline A, David chooses to stay in Keilah and, because God knows how the people of the town will choose, he gets turned over to Saul, and most likely dies.

In timeline B, David leaves town and therefore isn't available to be turned over to Saul.

God's foreknowledge of how the people of the town will choose IF David chooses Option A is just a small, simple example of something God does constantly on a mind-blowingly massive scale.

Now, I'm a terrible chess player. The game requires mentally imaging the possible moves of 30 pieces within a two-dimensional space of sixty-four squares. Some brains are wired for it. Mine is not one of them. Now let's think about God's brain . . . or mind . . . whatever He has going on there.

To *foreknow* is simply to "know before." I'm free to choose and make ten thousand choices a day. And God knows the choices I'll make because He knows me better than I know myself. And each one of those ten thousand choices each day alters the timeline of the future—sometimes in tiny ways, and sometimes in very big ways. (In the movie, *It's a Wonderful Life*, George Bailey sees an alternate timeline. One in which he'd never been born.)

It's not just that *my* choices constantly alter the future timeline of the planet. Your choices are doing the same thing, as are the choices of every living person on the planet. As a result, God is constantly "seeing" not just THE future, but every possible future, in real time.

But don't misunderstand, God is not passively sitting back watching what we decide. He is actively (sovereignly) shaping and guiding the unfolding of History because He is actively engaged with and working through His people.

The Adam and Eve narrative is about God choosing to have partners in the earth. His original program was to partner with them and their descendants in carrying out His wonderful plans and purposes on this planet. It still is. He influences hearts. He ...

Speaks.

Corrects.

Guides.

Empowers.

Helps.

God has declared the end from the beginning. Things ultimately turn out the way He has planned and intended. Yet He's smart enough to achieve those outcomes without violating His legal order, reneging on His covenant promises, or in any way violating His integrity. In other words, God won't cheat at the game He invented. He's playing by His own rules.

6

A 500-YEAR-OLD SOLUTION

What I've laid out for you here isn't exactly a new way of thinking about God's sovereignty. Back in the late 1500s, a Jesuit priest in Spain named Luis de Molina suggested pretty much the same thing. Molina, a brainiac professor at the University of Coimbra, lived in a time in which both Protestants and Catholics had factions squaring off on these issues. The Protestants had Calvinists and Arminians. The Roman Catholics had Augustinians and Thomists.

> In both cases, one of the opposing tribes represented "Team Sovereignty" and the other was "Team Free Will."

Molina suggested, correctly I think, that there should be a way to reconcile the seemingly contradictory biblical doctrines of God's sovereignty and His gift of free will to Man. His solution has come to be known as Molinism.

It's a 500-year-old solution very similar to what I've described for you here on these pages.

7

LET'S WRAP THIS ALL UP IN A TIDY PACKAGE, SHALL WE?

I have tried to lay the groundwork for a different way to think about what is widely called God's "sovereignty." I'm going to try to build on that foundation now.

I have a very smart friend who once wrote to me saying, "I have jettisoned the word 'sovereign' from my theological vocabulary. It's been misused so often and for so long that there is *always* the possibility of being misunderstood when people hear it."

I get it. The typical believer's conception of God's sovereignty on planet Earth lies somewhere between the powers displayed by Jim Carrey's character in *Bruce Almighty* and Samantha Stephens on the old sitcom *Bewitched*.

But as I've pointed out, this view doesn't account for Mankind's God-granted freedom to choose, nor the self-limiting nature of God's character in light of His legal grant of stewardship and dominion to Man. This creates that apparent paradox I mentioned before. I'll put it another way:

God can absolutely do anything He wants. But…

He's made some commitments. And…

He's utterly good, holy, and righteous. So…

He honors His commitments. Which…

Limits His freedom to some degree.

8

IS PRAYER A
MEANINGLESS EXERCISE?

T hose who believe that God is always getting His way
and that every outcome, no matter how horrific or
appalling, has been predetermined and preordained by
God, find themselves without much incentive to pray.
What's the point? (I'll address this issue directly before
I close.)

I believe the biblical path out of that paradox is to
make a distinction between what I call God's "Macro
Sovereignty" and the concept of "Micro Sovereignty."

The typical evangelical Christian on the street
assumes God is behind every event in her day—that He
is either the direct cause of the event or He "allows" the
event because it fits into His plan for her life. This is what

I call "micro sovereignty." It's a view of God's sovereignty that sees God's causative or allow-ative intentionality on every tiny particle of existence, including all the pain, abuse, trauma, and horror that life can bring. This includes all the hurtful choices others make because, in this view, free will is an illusion. This view has a name. There is a subset of Calvinist thought that calls this "Exhaustive Divine Determinism" or EDD for short. A lot of Christians have been taught some variant of this.

This theology often emerges after a tragedy. Well-intentioned believers offer it in the form of comfort to themselves or others after something heartbreaking has happened:

"His ways are higher than our ways."

"You just have to believe this happened for a reason."

And my personal favorite:

"God wanted to equip you to minister to other people who have had this same horrific thing happen to them."

Sound familiar? I trotted some version of these out myself on more than one occasion back in my younger days. Usually, the recipient of this brand of comfort is too polite or grief-shocked to challenge that logic with something like:

"Hold on. So God arranged for my kid to get hit by a drunk driver because He's allowing other people's kids to get hit by drunk drivers too? Therefore, they need ministry? But wait, He wouldn't need me to minister to these grief-stricken parents if He didn't "allow" those kids to be killed in the first place. Right? So . . . seriously . . . what the ever-loving hades."

There's another logic problem confronted by holders of one of the various versions of the micro-sovereignty paradigm:

Why pray? Seriously. Why?

If God is getting His preferred outcome at the micro level every second of every day, what is the point of praying? Why did Jesus, after the disciples requested a clinic in effective prayer, instruct them to pray: "Father . . . May your will be done on earth as it is in heaven"?

Why would Jesus repeatedly say,

"Ask the Father . . ."

"Whatever you ask the Father in my name . . ."

"Ask what you will . . ."?

(See: Matthew 18:19; Luke 11:13; John 14:13; 14:16; 15:16; 16:23; 16:26)

Some micro-sovereignty-ists have attempted to come up with an answer to that question. As I heard a preacher on the radio intone with great seriousness and conviction a while back: "Prayer doesn't change God. It changes us."

That sounds quite spiritual and profound when you first hear it. Then you think about the implications and it falls apart.

Of course, prayer doesn't change *God*. That's a red herring. The question is: Does prayer change *things*?

This view is basically saying that prayer is the spiritual equivalent of running on a treadmill: "You don't actually get anywhere but, hey, it's good for you!"

9

AN ALTERNATIVE VIEW

What if God's sovereignty is the "macro" variety?

What if God's micro sovereignty is, to some degree, limited by...His grant of free will to Man; His delegation of legal stewardship rights and authority to Man; and, most of all, by His own righteousness and character?

As I suggested earlier, God is self-limited by His own character—His just-ness prevents Him from violating the spiritual legal structure upon which He framed the universe and placed Man within it.

Nevertheless, the Bible is clear that God is moving History (capital "H") toward an end of His choosing. He has both foreknown and foreordained the way everything winds up. His intellect and power are so unimaginably vast that he can process the free choices of eight billion human inhabitants, the effects of a fallen creation, and the nefarious activities of a rogue, outlaw enemy and still fully accomplish His plans and purposes in the earth and faithfully fulfill the promise of Romans 8:28 to every believer.

What a mighty, extraordinary God who can do that!

Adopting the paradigm I outlined above causes much of the paradoxical confusion and contradiction to evaporate that so many Christians wrestle with. And it causes many previously mysterious passages of the Bible to suddenly make sense.

Why pray? Because God has chosen to *need* us to pray. Our asking God to move isn't an empty or meaningless exercise. It opens legal/judicial windows through which He can move provision, power, and outcomes. It is the revelation behind Charles Wesley's admission:

> "The longer I go in this faith, the more convinced I am that God does nothing except in response to believing prayer."[2]

It is the reality behind Jesus' words in the Model Prayer: "Father … your kingdom come, your will be done on earth as it is in heaven." Why would Jesus tell us to pray that way if God always gets His preferred outcome whether we pray or not? The stunning truth is that God chose to build a world in which He'd need human partners to accomplish all of His good plans and purposes. Which is precisely why God's bitter, outcast enemy immediately looked to hijack and hoodwink God's chosen partners. And it's why God spent thousands of years methodically working to recover what had been hijacked by getting Jesus, another "Adam," into the earth.

You have likely heard the encouraging phrase "All God's promises to us are 'yes' and 'amen'." That's a paraphrase of 2 Corinthians 1:20. Actually, it's a mis-paraphrase of that verse. Let's look at it in the very literal *New American Standard Bible* translation:

> *For as many as the promises of God are, **in Him** [**Jesus**] *they are yes; therefore **through Him** [**Jesus**] *also is our Amen to the glory of God through us.* (ADDITIONS AND EMPHASIS MINE)

This verse is describing a two-sided equation. On one side, God looks at all the promises He has made to His New Covenant people, the Church, then looks at Jesus at says, "Yes! Jesus fully qualifies to receive all of them. He has met every condition and completely fulfilled every obligation. To all those promises I say, yes!"

But this equation is incomplete. On the other side sits little you and little me.

One of the most amazing miracles of the "new birth" is that, in some mystical sense, we are baptized into Jesus. (Romans 6:3; Galatians 3:27) This produces a state in which we are "in Him" and He is "in us." Which is why the second half of that verse says, "...therefore through Him also is our Amen ..." In other words, because we are "in Jesus" we are able to hear God's "yes" and respond with a confident, faith-filled "Amen!"

Do you see it? This is describing a partnership. It's a two-sided recipe. And, at the end of the verse, we discover what happens when the two vital ingredients— God's "yes" and our "amen"—are combined.

It is "…to the glory of God…"

And how is this
glory manifested?

"…through us."

It's stunning to contemplate. And this will sorely vex many theologians in numerous camps. But God designed a system of partnership in which a lot of stuff happens only if one or more of His partners (us) participates and gives voice to what He wants spoken or does what He wants done.

Now let's wind this down.

10

THE CORNERSTONE OF OUR FAITH

One of the most frequently repeated phrases in all of the Bible is this song of praise:

> *Oh, give thanks to the* LORD, ***for He is good!***
> *For His mercy endures forever.* (EMPHASIS MINE)

It first appears in 1 Chronicles 16:34. It reappears in various forms in 1 Chron. 16:41; II Chron. 5:13; Psalm 100:5; Psalm 107:1; Psalm 118:1; Psalm 118:29; and Psalm 136:1; Psalm 145:9; Jer. 33:11; and Nahum 1:7.

There is scarcely another phrase in all the Bible as frequently repeated as "The Lord is good." Perhaps we should take note of that.

Faith and trust in the utter goodness of God is the cornerstone of a stable, mature faith. That means not wrongly laying the blame for

tragedy,

heartache,

and atrocity

at His feet.

On the contrary, the Father has paid a horrific price to patiently unfold a plan to undo Man's free-will mistake that unleashed all this heartache.

Which brings us back to the conundrum Martin Bashir asked Rob Bell . . . the Bashir-Bell Paradox.

Remember, Bashir challenged:

A: God is all-powerful but doesn't care about the people of Japan, and therefore they're suffering.

—Or—

B: He does care about the people of Japan but is not all-powerful.

If you've hung with me to this point, I suspect you now know how I would respond to that challenge:

"Mr. Bashir, your use of the term 'all-powerful' indicates you have a common but cartoonish conception of God's latitude to act in a fallen, broken world. But I can assure you that He cares desperately about the Japanese people. And there's no message in the earthquake and no lesson in the tsunami. God delivered His message on a barren hillside outside of Jerusalem roughly 2,000 years ago."

11

"STOP. IT."

Several years ago, I came across a heartfelt and transparent essay by ESPN writer and host, Jason Wilde. In it, Wilde opened up about battling darkness and depression after he and his wife lost a baby about halfway through the pregnancy. In it, without anger or bitterness, he mentioned how profoundly unhelpful it was to have well-meaning Christians (he is not one) come up to him and try to help by saying things like, "God only gives you as much as you can handle."

I recall being deeply saddened by hearing that. I was probably more than a little angry as well because I immediately wrote a cranky, scoldy social media post that read:

"Fellow Christians of planet earth: Stop trying to comfort the grieving by saying 'God will never give you more than you can handle.' It's garbage theology. And it's not comforting. Stop. It."

I meant that, and here's why. The advice (falsely) positions God as the great cosmic dispenser of misery and suffering. What's worse, it depicts Him as carefully monitoring just how much misery and suffering we each can handle without completely collapsing under the weight of it all, to keep Himself from over-doing it.

It encourages us to imagine Him viewing our "misery capacity" as some sort of dashed line at the top of a measuring cup. Should our capacity to handle heartache increase a bit . . . well, then God is surely there with an eyedropper of pain ready to add more until we're topped off, but never to the point that it rises above the line.

It's hard to count how many ways this is wrong. But, in the light of everything you've read so far, let me hit a few of the highlights.

1.   It misidentifies the source of evil and suffering.

We live in a fallen creation filled with fallen humans operating with the power of free will. The flooded home, the miscarried pregnancy, the child lost to the drunk driver, the housewife with the swollen black eye, the stolen iPhone, and the irritable bowel ... all of these, and an endless list of other heartaches and headaches, are a result of either the one (broken creation) or the other (broken people). And, of course, there's God's despicable, raging enemy, Satan, who is actively at work in and through both.

2.   God is all about healing pain, not causing it. Restoring, not destroying.

Jesus told us that if we've seen Him, we've seen the Father. (John 14:9) He said that He only did the things He saw the Father doing. (John 5:19) Thus, it's revealing that Jesus broke up every funeral He ever came across; healed every person who requested it. Wherever He encountered human suffering, He relieved it.

He said the thief (Satan) comes only to steal, kill, and destroy. But that He had come to provide abundant life. (John 10:10)

3. It distorts the truth about God's sovereignty.

The sad young man from ESPN really believes God took the life of his baby. And every would-be comforter who offered up, "This was part of God's plan," or "He won't give you more than you can handle," seems to agree. "Yep. God did this to you," they're affirming. "But cheer up. It's all for the best!"

As we've seen on the preceding pages, one of the most common and disastrous theological concepts loose in the world is that child's cartoon view of God's sovereignty that suggests that God is getting exactly what He wants every second of every day in every place on planet Earth.

Dear friend, He isn't.

A lost, hurting, dying world is understandably reluctant to run to a God who they believe to be the author of their deepest pain. But that's simply not an accurate picture of who He is or why they've been hurt.

He is good. And He has gone to extraordinary lengths, at unspeakable personal cost, to meet us at the point of our suffering and offer healing and hope.

Perhaps the next time an unbeliever has his or her heart shattered by loss, a more comforting (and more theologically sound) response might be:

"I'm so sorry that happened. How painful that must be. Let me walk through this with you. And please know that you can take that pain to a God who loves you. Because He's not your problem. He's your only hope for healing."

The same is true for you. You can confidently join the ancient chorus of voices on earth and in heaven singing:

"Oh, give thanks to the Lord,
for He is good.
And His mercies endure forever."

TL;DR

- God is good. Utterly, completely good.
- Suffering and heartache and tragedy are a part of our reality because we're living in a broken world filled with broken people who have been gifted with free will.
- Because God legally delegated dominion over the planet to mankind, He is constrained by His own righteousness and integrity from violating free will or working independently from human partners. He doesn't cause calamity. He doesn't even "allow" calamity.

- Romans 8:28 doesn't say God causes all things— period. It says, "He causes all things *to work together* for the good of His people." He's that good and that brilliant.
- God doesn't just know the future. He knows all possible futures because He knows how every single person will choose in every situation in every one of those possible futures.
- Prayer is not only meaningful but vital because God has chosen to *need* us.
- With this knowledge, and working with His partners in the earth, the Church, He is working History to the ends He has purposed from the very beginning.

ABOUT THE AUTHOR

David A. Holland is a writer, speaker, teacher, husband, father, and grandfather—carrying a call to help God's people better comprehend His extraordinary goodness and extravagant grace.

His writing on faith, life, and culture—along with a wide array of other resources—is accessible at:

DAVIDAHOLLAND.COM

X: @DavidHolland

Instagram: @DavidAHolland

Facebook: /DavidAHolland.Inspires

YouTube: @DavidAHolland

ENDNOTES

1   https://www.msnbc.com/martin-bashir/watch/questioning-heaven-and-hell-45149251526

2   John Wesley, *How to Pray: The Best of John Wesley on Prayer*, (2007), Barbour

www.ingramcontent.com/pod-product-compliance
Lightning Source LLC
Chambersburg PA
CBHW051648120626
46551CB00015B/2261